Charleston's Gullah Recipes

By Chef Darren

Gullah Recipes

Greetings everyone, my name is Chef Darren Campbell. I was born and raised in Charleston, SC. For most of my early childhood I grew up eating traditional foods that my grandmother from Edisto Island, SC prepared.

I began thinking about writing a Gullah cookbook ever since I was nineteen living in the Washington DC area. My Aunt Debbie prepared a pot of red rice for me to take to my company's Christmas party. Everyone at the party was amazed at the color and taste. Most of them had never heard of or eaten red rice before. They could not figure how she made the rice red. I gave them the recipe and they wanted to know about other Gullah dishes. So here I am many years later writing this book.

Table of Contents

Edited by Francine Jenkins
©2025 The Simone Club
All Rights Reserved
For more info:
www.gullahrecipes.com
www.palmettoblend.com

3

The Gullah People

The Gullah people are directly descended from the enslaved that lived and labored on the rice plantations of the Low Country regions of South Carolina and Georgia, which includes both the coastal plains and the chain of Sea Islands, which runs parallel to the coast.

Gullah slaves were different from slaves in other parts of America. Tropical diseases caused many Southern planters to move their homes far away from the fields and had little contact with their slaves. The Gullah had built up a resistance to many of these diseases while White folks would often get very sick and sometimes die. Therefore, many rice plantations were ran by a few White overseers and Black folks called drivers.

Because of their isolation and strong community life, the Gullah people were able to preserve more of their African cultural heritage than any other groups of Black Americans. African art, food and dialect are still alive through the Gullah people today.

The Gullah language, sometimes called the Geechee language, is based on English with strong influences from West and Central African languages. The Gullah people speak a Creole language similar to Sierra Leone and surrounding areas.

The Gullah people are famous for their delicious foods, seasonings and recipes based on the crops they traditionally grew. Some of these recipes are have been past down for centuries.

The Rice Crop

It all began by accident when, in 1685, a storm-battered ship sailing from Madagascar wobbled into the Charles Town harbor.

The ship captain gave the colonists a small quantity of "Golden Seed Rice" (named for its color to repay them for repairs to the ship).

The low-lying marshlands bordered by fresh tidal water rivers of the Carolinas and Georgia proved to be ideal for rice production.

Carolina Gold, which emanated from Africa, became a commercial staple grain in the coastal lands of Charles Town, SC.

Rice was called "the best opportunity for industrial profit which 18th century America afforded."

Rice was in big demand in Europe and very expensive to import from the Orientals.

By 1690, Africans from West Africa were in Charles Town cultivating the rice crop. By 1700, rice was established as a major crop for the colonists. That year 300 tons of American rice, referred to as "Carolina Gold Rice," was shipped to England.

By 1726, the Port of Charlestown was exporting about 4,500 metric tons of "Carolina Golden," which later became the standard of high-quality rice throughout the world.

By 1730, the Gullah people were two-thirds of Charlestown's population.

Red Rice

Grandma Bessie's

I remember watching my grandmother making Red Rice and fish or chicken dinners every Friday to raise money for the Church.

Red rice is my favorite dish and is one of the harder dishes to get right. You either use too much water and your rice looks like oatmeal or you cook it too high and dry it out. The key to a good pot of Red Rice is measurements. You will also have to do a little stirring and use different temperatures. Through lots of trials and errors, I finally got it right. I have learned how to make my Grandma Bessie's Red Rice.

Cooking time: 60 minutes, plus 10 minutes to prep Feeds 6-8 people

Ingredients

2 ½ cups Carolina Gold rice or 1 ¼ cup parboiled rice and 1 cup white rice
2 tsp of Palmetto Blend or 1 tsp sea salt and 1 tsp ground black pepper
(*season to taste*) 1 stalk celery, a small tomato, 1bell pepper, 1 onion
(chop into big pieces) 1 lb of Meat cut into big pieces (beef or turkey sausage)
1 cup of tomato sauce and ½ cup of stewed tomatoes;
¼ cup vegetable oil
2 cups of water
¼ cup sugar

Directions: Turn large size pot on medium high and add vegetable oil. Add meat, cook until brown and add bell pepper, celery and onion. Stir fry for 8 minutes. Add in tomato sauce, water, seasonings, sugar, and stewed tomatoes. Stir mixture, add rice and tomato, turn stove down to medium, stir and cover for 8 minutes. Pour mixture in baking pan and cover with foil. Oven should be preheated to 390 degrees and cook 40-45 minutes. *For stovetop stir twice, most of the sauce should be absorbed. Turn stove down to simmer. Simmer for 45-50 minutes or until done. Stir and serve.*

Chicken Purlieu

I was in Atlanta, Georgia in 2008 promoting one of my books on a radio show. The radio DJ asked the name of that dish he had in Charleston that mixed the chicken and the rice together. He said, "Man that was the best thing I ever tasted."

Cooking time:
70 minutes
Feeds 8-10 people
Ingredients
1 whole chicken
2 tbsp of **Palmetto Blend** or
1 tbsp of pepper and
1 tbsp of salt
(season to taste)
1 large onion cut into chunks
2 stalks of celery chunks
1 med green bell pepper
¼ stick of butter
5 cups of water
3 cups of white rice

Directions
Wash chicken on both sides and inside. Remove chicken neck and butt and discard. Heat large saucepan on high, add water, ½ of seasonings, and ½ of vegetables. Bake on 400 for 25-30 minutes until meat is falling off bone. *You can also boil or pressure-cook the chicken.* Using two forks, separate meat from the bone. Preheat oven to 400 degrees. Place meat in large baking pan. Add additional seasoning and vegetables. Add five cups of chicken broth made from the cooked chicken. Pour broth over chicken. Add 3 cups of rice. Stir, add butter and place lid or foil over pan and secure corners so rice can steam. Bake for 35-45 until rice is fluffy. Stir and enjoy.

Okra Purlieu

I still call to mind the drive down that bumpy dirt road leading to my great grandparent's house in Edisto Island. My Mom told me she remembered a lake on their farm growing up. Years later, my Cousin Julius told me that he and Cousin Joseph farmed rice from that lake when they were boys. Cousin Julius is nicknamed the "Okra man" because he grows and prepares many okra dishes. My favorite is the **Fried Okra Rice** that he makes during our family reunions.

Cooking time:
30 minutes
Feeds 4-6 people
Ingredients
2 lbs Fresh Okra
1 lbs beef bacon or sausage
½ stick of butter or olive oil
1 tbsp of **Palmetto Blend** or ½ tbsp of pepper and ½ tbsp of salt (season to taste)
1 small onion cut into chunks
3 cups of cooked white rice
1 small tomato

Okra was brought to America from West Africa by the Gullah people.

Directions: Cook rice while okra is being prepared. Heat stove to med high. In a large frying pan, cook sausage until brown on one side. Flip over and add onions. Heat until sausage and onion are cooked. Move mixture to one side of pan and add okra and butter. Add seasoning and water if needed. Cook for 10-15 minutes or until okra gets slightly tender. Move mixture to one side of pan. Add rice and butter. Mix together until rice turns brown. Garnish with sliced tomato.

Hoppin' John

Hoppin John is a traditional New Year's Day cuisine. Served with greens, fried chicken, and macaroni and cheese, my mom made this dinner ever since I remember. Friends and family members have requested this plate on birthdays and graduations because it is too good to have just one day out of the year.

Directions: Add water to a large saucepan, bring to a boil, and add smoked meat, field peas, and seasoning. Boil on med high for 1 ½ hours or until meat is tender, beans are soft inside and gravy is dark. To save time you may pressure cook for 40 to 55 minutes. Stir and check on while boiling. Be careful not to cook on high because beans can stick to the pot quickly.

Cooking time: 90 minutes

Feeds 6 -8 people

Ingredients

1 lb of bag of dry field peas
1½ lbs of smoked meat (smoked turkey wings, or necks
1 tsp of salt and black pepper
1 tsp of Palmetto Blend (season to taste)
½ diced onion and 2 bay leaves
3 cups of white rice or mix with parboiled rice
12-16 cups of water

Separate meat from peas and place meat in a med deep baking pan. Preheat oven to 375 degrees. Measure how much cups of peas and gravy is in the pot and add to baking pan. Add 1 cup of rice for every 1½ cup of peas and gravy. For example, 4½ cups of peas and gravy would require 3 cups of rice. Pour and stir evenly peas, gravy, and rice into baking pan with meat. Place foil over pan and bake for 45-50 minutes until rice is ready. Stir and serve.

In and Around Charleston

11

Baked Chicken

Baked chicken is easy to make and tastes great. It's a dish you can just put in the oven and let it do what it does.

Directions: Soak chicken in vinegar for ten minutes and rinse with water. Let dry, add seasoning on both sides. Place chicken, chopped onion, celery, bell pepper and two bay leaves into a baking dish. Add 1 cup water (Optional) for every pound of chicken. Bake on 400 for 35 min, flip chicken over, add sliced potatoes and bake for 30 min until chicken is golden brown.

Cooking time: 65 minutes
Feeds 5-6 people
Ingredients

1 whole chicken (8 pieces) or chicken parts
¼ cup of Palmetto Blend Seasoning or 1 tbsp of black pepper and 2 tbsp of salt (season to taste)
2 bay leaves
1 large onion cut into chunks
2 stalks of celery cut into chunks
1 green bell pepper cut into chunks
2 med potatoes
1 cup of warm water

Stewed Chicken

Seconds please, is what friends always say after they had a taste of my legendary stew chicken. The secret to good tasting stew chicken is to use the whole chicken (both dark and white meat). That way the chicken would never be too greasy or too dry.

Cooking time: 50 minutes

Feeds 5-6 people

Ingredients

1 whole chicken (8 pieces)
¼ cup of Palmetto Blend Seasoning or
1 tbsp of black pepper and 2 tbsp of salt (season to taste)
1/3 cup of oil
1/3 cup of flour
2 bay leaves
1 large onion cut into chunks
2 stalks of celery cut into chunks
1 green bell pepper cut into chunks
6 cups of warm water

Directions

Wash chicken with water let dry and add seasoning on both sides. Heat large saucepan on medium high and add oil. When oil is hot, add seasoned chicken and bay leaves. Fry on one side for 15 minutes. Turn chicken pieces over, cook other-side for 10 minutes, and then add celery, bell pepper, and onion chunks. Stir and cook 10 minutes. Drain excess oil. Mix 1 cup of warm water with flour, mix until flour dissolves. Add flour mixture to chicken and vegetable mixture and stir. Cook for 10 minutes. (For thicker gravy, add more flour) Turn stove down to medium low and stir and cook for an additional 10 to 20 minutes. Serve over white rice with corn or string beans.

Southern Fried Chicken

When people think of the South, they think about fried chicken, and no one made it better than my Great grandma. It was crunchy on the outside and flavorful inside. Every bite made me want more.

Directions: Wash chicken with water let dry and add seasoning on both sides. For extra crispy chicken, scramble one large egg, milk or mustard and dip before seasoning. Heat large pan on medium to medium high and add oil. Mix flour in a large *paper bag*. Place four or five pieces of chicken in bag and shake to cover both sides. When oil is hot, shake excess flour off chicken and add to skillet. Cook on one side for 20 minutes. Chicken should be golden brown before turning. Cook other side for 15 minutes or until chicken floats on top of oil indicating chicken is fully cooked. Sometimes sticking a fork in the chicken when frying to make sure the inside is fully cooked is a good idea.

Cooking time:
45 minutes
Feeds 5-6
people
Ingredients
3 lbs of
chicken
or 8 pieces
3 tbsp of
Palmetto
Blend or black
pepper and salt
(season to taste)
2 cups of oil, 1 ½ cup of flour,
1 egg or ½ cup milk or mustard
for extra crispy

Season your plates with Gullah inspired seasoning!

"I created Palmetto Blend while I was writing this cookbook.

I wanted to make an authentic tasting blend that people could use on all their dishes."

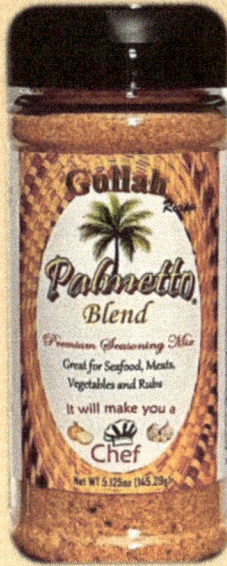

Chef Darren

Cook like a Chef!

"It's my Favorite!"

The Gullah people are famous for making food with love and seasoned to perfection. Palmetto Blend Seasoning combines the perfect measurements of 7 all natural spices.

Great for barbecues!

Local Fish

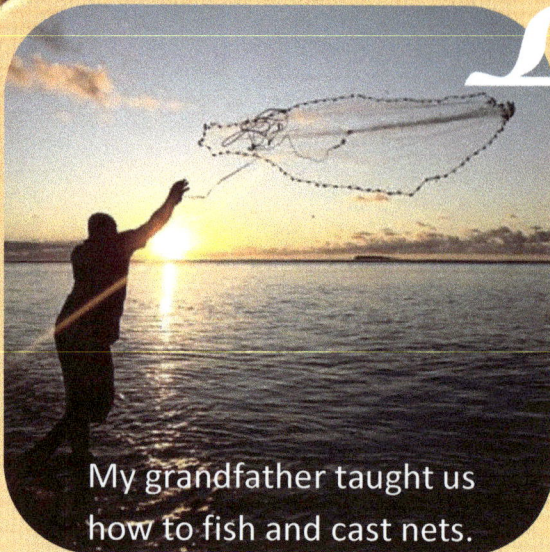

My grandfather taught us how to fish and cast nets.

Grandfather James would wake my brother and me up at 4 A.M. to accompany him when he went fishing on the river. I often think of him casting that big old net into the water. He would walk into the river about knee high. He threw that net as far as he could, then he would shake the net into a bucket.

There is nothing fresher than the Catch of the Day!

Whiting

Sheepshead

Speckled Trout

Sea Bass

Red Snapper

Flounder

Whatsoever hath fins and scales in the waters, in the seas, and in the rivers, them shall you eat. *Leviticus 11:9*

Fish Fry

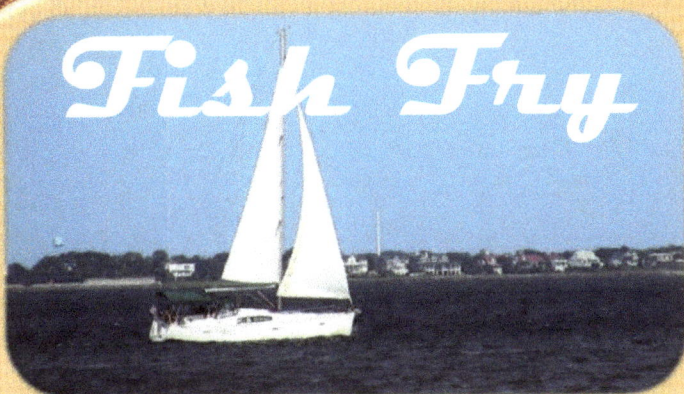

Charleston is famous because of our delicious food. You can smell the aroma of the fish frying blocks away. When I was growing up, they cooked the whole fish with head on. My son in law, Isim made us this fish dinner on Sunday.

Directions: Heat large pan on medium high and add oil. Wash, dry and evenly season both sides of fish. Place seasoned fish and onion in pan cook for seven minutes on both sides. Slide fish to one side of pan and fry onion and flour on the other. When flour is brown, add water, stir and simmer for 15 minutes. Serve over grits or rice.

Fried Fish

Cooking time: 20 min

Ingredients: 2 lbs of fish
2 tbsp Palmetto Blend Seasoning mix or 1 tbsp of black pepper and salt (season to taste)
1 cup of cooking oil
1 ½ cup flour and ¼ cup of cornmeal.

Directions

Heat large pan on medium high and add oil. Wash and evenly season both sides of fish. Put flour and cornmeal in bag. Place seasoned fish in bag and shake until both sides are fully covered. Place fish in hot pan. Cook 7 minutes on each side or until golden brown.

Fish and Gravy

Cooking time: 30 minutes

Ingredients: 2 lbs of fish
2 tbsp Palmetto Blend mix or black pepper and sea salt. (season to taste)
¼ cup of cooking oil
½ sliced onion, 1 tbsp of flour and ¾ cup water.

17

Fish and Grits

You can fry it, bake it, broil it, or grill it. It does not matter how you cook it, fish over grits is a Gullah staple. It is one of my favorite things to eat for breakfast!

Corn is grinded to make grits

Fish and Grits

Cooking time: 15-20 minutes (Feeds 3-4 people)

Ingredients:

2 lbs of fish

2 tbsp Palmetto Blend Seasoning mix or1 tbsp of black pepper and sea salt (season to taste)

¼ cup of cooking oil (Olive oil) and 2 tbsp of butter

1 ½ cup of grits

3 cups water

Directions

Heat large pan on medium high and add oil and 1 tbsp of butter. Rinse, dry with napkin and evenly season both sides of fish. Place fish on skin side on hot pan. Sear for ten minutes or until brown and flip over. Add more oil and butter if needed. Sear an additional five to ten minutes until brown.

Grits: Add water, butter and salt if needed to medium size pot. Allow water to boil and add grits. Cook on med-high for five to ten minutes and stir until grits thickens.

Baked Fish Directions, Heat oven to 375. Add oil on bottom of large baking pan. Rinse, dry with napkin and evenly season both sides of fish. Place fish, skin side down in pan. Add butter on top of fish. Place in oven for 25 minutes or until golden brown.

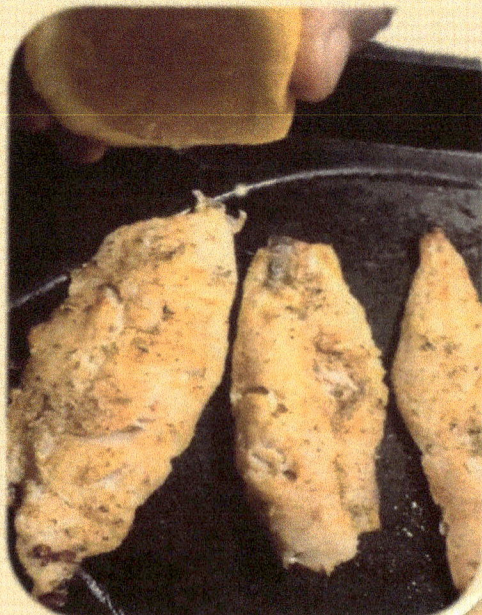

Tuna Salad

Tuna or Salmon salad has been a tradition in Charleston for many years. At weddings, parties and local events this dish is one of the most requested and if it is prepared correctly, the first to go. I got this recipe from my friend April, who is well known because of this dish.

Cooking time: 35 minutes
Feeds 8-10 people
Ingredients
1.5lbs Tuna Fish or Salmon
½ chopped onion, 1 tomato
1 bell pepper
4 boiled eggs
3 scallions
chopped
1 tbsp Palmetto
Blend or ½ tbsp
of pepper and
salt (season to taste)
16 oz pasta noodles
1 lb mayonnaise
2 tbsp of thousand Island

Directions: Heat 4 cups of water on high in a medium size saucepan. Add eggs and noodles and cook for 20 min or until noodles are tender. Separate eggs from noodles, and place noodles in freezer for 15 min to cool.

Mix pasta noodles with tuna, shelled eggs, onions, bell pepper, tomatoes and seasoning. Blend mayonnaise and Thousand Island dressing together and mix with pasta. Let cool for 30mins and serve.

19

Oxtail

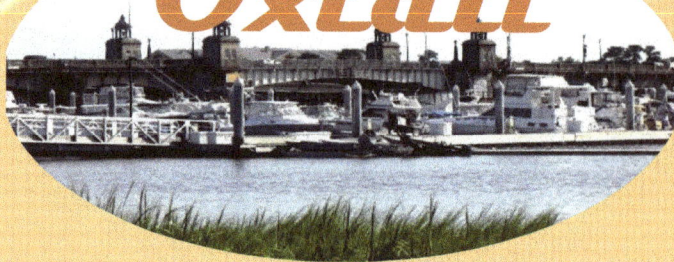

My Grandmother was in the kitchen cooking dinner every night of the week. I grew up spoiled eating delicious home cooked meals almost every day. One of our monthly treats was Oxtail. It can be pricy so we would only have it occasionally which made it all the better. I got this recipe from my cousin Nakiesha who cooks a *mean* Oxtail.

Preheat oven to 350 degrees

Rub the ox tails in house seasoning

Heat the oil in a large pan on top of stove, sear the oxtails on all sides, then put aside in a large roasting pan. Place items #4-13 in roasting pan and spoon sauce over tails, Cover tightly with aluminum foil and cook for 2 hours and 15 minutes (can use a pressure cooker for 45-60 minutes to save time). Remove from oven, put red potatoes and carrots into roasting pan, stir, and recover. Cook for additional 30-45 minutes so vegetables can cook. Once done, stir, and serve over hot rice.

Ingredients:

1. 2lbs ox tails
2. House Seasoning (salt, black pepper, garlic powder) with Palmetto Blend (season to taste)
3. 1 tsp oil (olive oil *fine*)
4. 8-10 oz of beef broth
5. 5 oz red cooking wine
6. 1 tbsp Worcestershire
7. 4 oz tomato sauce
8. 1 tsp hot sauce
9. 1 onion, sliced
10. 4 large garlic cloves
11. 1 tsp dried oregano
12. 1 tsp dried basil
13. 3 bay leaves
14. 4-6 red potatoes *cut into wedges*
15. 4 carrots cut into wedges

Beef Stew

When I say my Aunt Debbie's beef stew is good, I mean it is fantastic! Even my grandma gave her two thumbs up. Debbie is a good cook, however when it comes to her beef stew, she is a master chef.

Cooking time: 1.5 hours

Feeds 5-6 people

Ingredients

1 ½ lbs of Beef
stew chunks
1tbsp of flour
1 tbsp of Palmetto Blend Seasoning
mix or ½ tbsp each of black pepper
and of sea salt (season to taste)
½ large red onion, 4-5 potato's *red or
white,* 10 small carrots,
2 stalks of celery cut into chunks,
2 garlic cloves cut into small cubes,
1 bell pepper cut into chunks,
1 pack of beef bouillon powder
1 tsp Worcestershire sauce
8 oz of stewed tomatoes,
8 oz tomato sauce
¼ cup of oil,
24 oz of beef stock,
or 24 oz of water.
Add water
as needed.

Directions

Set beef at room temperature to cook evenly. Pat with paper towel to remove any dampness. (Do not wet) Season beef cubes. Place oil in a large stock pot on med high. Add beef cubs, onion, garlic and celery. Sauté until beef is brown evenly, don't cook to long. (*Remember it will cook in the soup*) Reduce stove to medium and remove half of the beef sauté. Remove excess oil (leave a little oil to mix with flour). Add flour to oil and 24 oz beef stock or 24 oz of water. Put beef sauté back in stew pot. Add tomato sauce, stewed tomatoes, bouillon and Worcestershire. Bring to a boil.

Cook for 25 minutes, add water as needed. Stir often to make sure stew doesn't stick. Add carrots and potatoes, cook for 10 more minutes. Reduce to low, and simmer for 30-40 minutes.

21

Turkey Wings

Turkey Wings is a weekly favorite in my house. It is simple to make and always appetizing. Turkey wings and gravy served over white rice and field peas is one of my children's favorite meals.

Cooking time: 55 minutes
Feeds 4-5 people

Ingredients

3 lbs of turkey wings
3 tbsp of Palmetto Blend Seasoning mix or ½ tbsp of black pepper and 1½ tbsp of sea salt (season to taste)
1 large onion cut into chunks
½ bell pepper cut into chunks
2 stalks of celery cut into chunks
2 bay leaves
5 cups of water

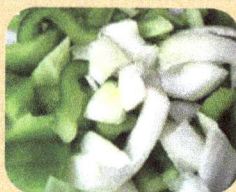

Turkey Wings over white rice with field peas

Directions

Wash turkey on both sides. Heat large saucepan on high, add water, ½ of seasonings, and ½ of vegetables. Boil for 40- 55 minutes or until meat is tender. *You can also pressure cook for 30 minutes.* Preheat oven to 400 degrees. Place turkey pieces in large baking pan. Add additional seasoning and vegetables. Add 5 cups of broth made from the boiling turkey. Pour broth over turkey. Bake for 20 minutes and turn over and bake for an additional 15 minutes or until turkey is golden brown.

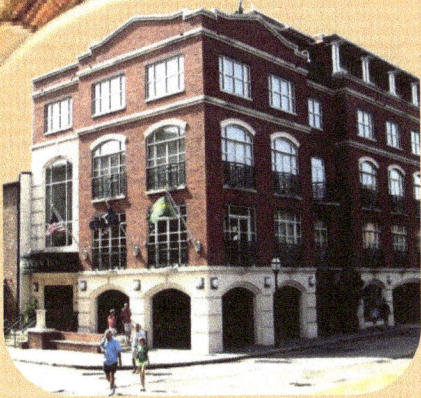

Smothered Steak

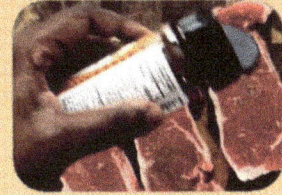

My father was a butcher at the local market so we grew up eating lots of steaks and roast. When I lived in Atlanta, my roommate Rio brought home some rib eye steaks. I smothered them in some gravy and served it on top of mashed potatoes. He said: "that was the most succulent steak I had ever tasted." The next week, I used the exact same recipe to make us some "succulent" smothered lamb chops.

Directions

Season both sides of steak or lamb. Heat large frying pan on medium high and add oil. When oil is hot, add seasoned meat and bay leaves. Fry on one side for 10 min. Turn pieces over; add bell pepper, and onion chunks. Cook other side for 10 minutes, adding mushrooms. Move steak to one side of pan and add flour to other side. Fry flour until brown. Add 1 ½ cup of water. Remove steak if needed for space, Turn stove down to med low. Turn steak over and cook for an additional 10 min.

Cooking time: 40 minutes Feeds 4-5 people

Ingredients

2 lbs of steak or lamb chop, ¼ cup of **Palmetto Blend** or 1 tbsp of black pepper and 2 tbsp spoon of salt (season to taste) 1 large onion cut into chunks, ½ bell pepper cut into chunks, 1 cup of sliced mushrooms, 2 bay leaves, 1 ½ cup of water, ½ cup of oil, and ½ cup of flour

Lima Beans

Lima bean served over white rice is another well-known Gullah dish that came over from the fields of West Africa. The word Lima is an African word and it is what I regularly order at Bertha's, my favorite soul food restaurant. I remember my Dad, Dan from Redtop, SC preparing this dish for our family every Wednesday.

Cooking time: 90 minutes
Feeds 6-8 people

Ingredients

16 oz bag of dry baby lima beans
1 lb of smoked meat (smoked turkey wings or necks
1 tbsp of black pepper
1 tbsp of Palmetto Blend or salt and pepper (season to taste)
3 bay leaves
6-8 cups of water

Directions

Add water to a large saucepan, bring to a boil, and add smoked meat, lima beans, bay leaves, and seasoning. Boil on med high for 1 ½ hours or until meat is tender, beans are soft inside and gravy is creamy. To save time you may pressure cook for 30 to 45 minutes. Stir and check on while boiling (add water as needed). Be careful not to cook on high because beans can stick to the pot quickly.

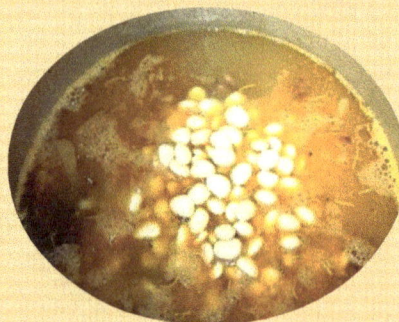

Collard Greens

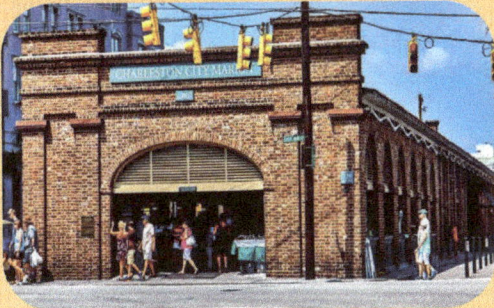

Collard greens with fried chicken and macaroni and cheese are a Sunday favorite in the South. We also eat this during holidays, reunions and receptions. Greens are the most famous and delectable of all the Gullah vegetables. Mother would serve it over white rice with chicken or turkey wings or beef roast. We also put vinegar or hot sauce over greens for extra zest.

Cooking time: 90 minutes
Feeds 6 -8 people

Ingredients

1 bunch of fresh collard greens, cut up or 1 bag of packaged greens
1 lb of smoked meat (smoked turkey, wings or necks)
½ tbsp of black pepper
add salt or Palmetto Blend as needed (season to taste)
6 cups of water or chicken broth

Directions

Add water or chicken broth to a large saucepan, bring to a boil, and add smoked meat and black pepper. Boil on med high for 1 hour or until meat is slightly tender. To save time you may pressure cook for 30 to 40 minutes. Stir and check on while boiling. Wash greens and place on top of meat and cook for an additional 35 minutes or until greens are tender. Once greens are tender, stir in with meat and serve.

Cabbage

It had been over thirty years before I rediscovered the magnificent flavor of cabbage. As a kid there were many vegetables I did not like. Cabbage was one of them. It looked somewhat like greens, which I loved, however it tasted very different. I never gave it another chance until I was visiting my friend Kim's house and cabbage was the main course. I knew I did not like cabbage but I said I would pretend to like it and eat the chicken. However, to my amazement, not only I liked it, I asked for seconds.

Cooking time:
30 minutes
Feeds 4 -6 people

Ingredients
1 head of cabbage
¼ cup of oil
½ lb beef or turkey bacon or *sausage*
1 tbsp of Palmetto Blend or black pepper and salt (season to taste)
1 tbsp of sugar

Directions
Rinse cabbage with water and cut cabbage into medium size shreds. Heat stove to med high and add oil to a large pan or wok. After oil is hot add meat. Cook until almost done and add cabbage and seasoning.

Leave on med high and stir fry for 15 minutes or until cabbage is moist but still kind of firm and crunchy. Simmer for 10 min and serve over rice with chicken or steak. Sometimes people add corned beef to the cabbage to add more taste or to replace a meat.

Okra Soup

I've seen okra soup cooked many ways. Some like it with corn, while others like it mixed with beans and vegetables. One of my cousins put cooked chicken in hers. My mom and aunt cook it with tomatoes, and smoked turkey wings.

Cooking time: 60 minutes

Ingredients

1 lb of ¼ inch cut okra
1 lb of *smoked m*eat (smoked turkey, wings or necks or sausage, chicken or beef. (Optional)
½ sliced onion
1 tbsp of each of salt and black pepper or 2 tbsp Palmetto Blend (season to taste)
6 cups of water or chicken broth
8 oz stewed tomato
15 oz tomato sauce
1 tbsp of sugar

Okra

Directions: Add water or chicken broth to a large saucepan; bring to a boil, and add meat and seasonings. Boil on med high until meat is tender. Add okra and onions to meat. Bring to a boil and add tomato sauce, sliced or stewed tomato and sugar. Add water if necessary. Place lid on top, cook on med high for 20 min and simmer until okra is tender or to your desire.

Okra

Cook 8 oz lima beans with meat (beans should be tender inside) Cook 6 corncob halves for 10 minutes. Drain and mix with okra soup. Cook for an additional 10 minutes.

Stir Fried Okra

It was love at first bite! This delicious blend of fresh okra, vegetables and meat will have your mouth dancing! My Dad's mother who everyone called "Sister" made it the best. The first time, I was around eight years old and my mother and I was visiting Sister. She gave us a bowl of Okra over white rice and the love affair began.

Sister was a real Gullah speaking woman who enjoyed cooking and sharing with everyone who came by her house.

Directions: Heat large skillet on medium high and add beef sausage and 1/8 cup of oil. When sausage is ready to turn, add vegetables, 1 tsp of Palmetto Blend Seasoning or ½ tsp of salt and pepper. Cook for 10 minutes. Add okra, seasoning and butter. Heat for an additional 10 until okra is tender. *"I love okra with fish."*

Cooking time: 35 minutes
Feeds 5-6 people
Ingredients
1 lb chopped Okra
1 sliced tomato and onion
2 bell peppers (Green -Yellow)
2 stalks of celery
½ pound of beef sausage
¼ cup oil or butter
2 tsp of Palmetto Blend or
1 tsp of salt and black pepper
   Season to taste!

Potato Salad

Cooking time: 60 minutes
Feeds 8 -10 people

Ingredients

3 lbs of potato
5 boiled eggs
2 stalks of celery
1 cup of mayonnaise
1 tsp mustard
½ onion & ½ bell pepper
4 cut stems of green onion
¾ cup of sweet diced pickles
1 tsp of black pepper
1 tsp of Palmetto Blend
(season to taste)

Directions:

Rinse and cut potatoes into cubes. In a large sauce pan, add water and bring to a boil. Add potato cubs (may also use red potatoes). Cook for 15-20 minutes until the cubes are slightly tender. Add diced onion, celery, bell peppers, eggs, green onions, mustard, mayo, seasoning and pickles. Mix together and sprinkle paprika or Palmetto Blend on top. Cover with foil and refrigerate until cool.

I invited a close friend of the family to a party we were having and he ask if we were cooking or was it going to be catered? He said even if my brother was cooking toast, he was going to be there. Marion has been cooking up dishes for many years; however salads are his specialty.

29

Macaroni and Cheese

Sunday dinner is not complete without the macaroni and cheese. Mom still saves me the pot after she mixes the macaroni. Her homemade macaroni and cheese taste a lot different from store bought or boxed. My cousin Starr added her own twist that makes her Mac and Cheese even more delicious. This is how real macaroni and cheese should taste.

Directions: Add water to a large saucepan; bring to a boil, and add noodles. Boil for 10 minutes or until noodles are slightly tender. Drain water and mix butter or margarine, egg and milk together. Add 6 oz cheddar cheese and stir together. Preheat oven to 375. Pour half in small baking pan. Put more cheese in middle and pour remaining mixture on top. Add the remaining cheese on top with a sprinkle of paprika. Bake for 25-30 minutes or until golden brown on top. **Macaroni and beef or chicken** is the best way to make this a meal. Just add ½ pound of cooked seasoned ground beef or chicken along with the cheese and bake. This was one of my favorite childhood meals.

Cooking time:
45 minutes
Feeds 6 -8 people
Ingredients
8 oz noodles
12 oz sharp cheese
10 oz evaporated milk
1 tsp mustard
4 tbsp butter
1 tsp of paprika
1 egg
1 tsp salt and pepper
(season to taste)

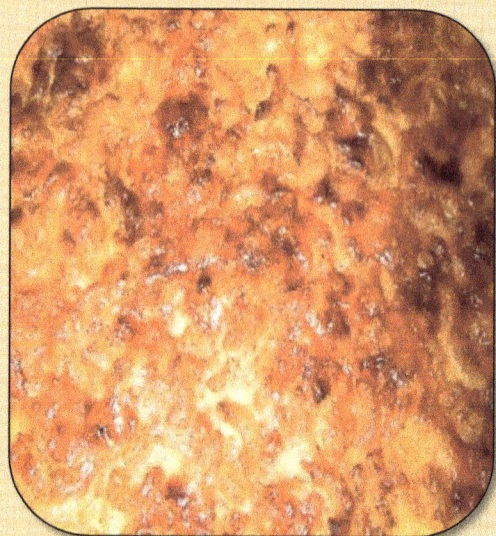

Pecan Chewies

Once you have tasted a Charleston Pecan Chewie there is no turning back. Your taste buds will be yearning for more. Just one will have you breathless and famished and the only cure is another. To some, chewies are the most delicious of all the Gullah treats. If you like pecans or walnuts than you will love chewies. My daughter Jessica uses Cousin Mildred's recipe to make it every time she visits.

Cooking time: 25 minutes
Feeds 6 -8 people
Ingredients
2 cups of light or dark brown sugar
3 whipped eggs
1 stick of butter
1 tsp of vanilla
2 ½ cup of self rising flour
1 cup of walnuts or pecans pieces
¼ cup of white powdered sugar

Directions:

In a med size bowl *cream* sugar and butter together. Mix in eggs, vanilla and flour. (Mixture will be thick) Stir in nuts. Grease and flour med size baking pan and spread mixture across pan. Cook for 20-25 minutes on 350 or until done in middle. Once cool, sprinkle powdered sugar over top and slice into 2 inch blocks.

In and Around Charleston

In and Around Charleston

33

Apple Pie

My cousin Mildred is well-known for sharing her tasty delights with friends and family. Anytime there is a special event you can find her pecan chewies or red velvet squares. So it was easy to ask her for a couple of her baking recipes.

Cooking time: 90 min

Feeds 6 -8 people

Ingredients

5-6 med size apples red or green

2 whipped eggs

1 cup of sugar (sweeten to taste)

1 stick of butter

1 tsp of vanilla

2 tsp of cinnamon

2 thick pie crust

Directions:

Peel and cut **apples or pears** into cubes. In a large sauce bowl, add soften butter, one egg, sugar, vanilla and cinnamon. Blend together and let soak for 60 minutes. Pour mixture into shelled pie crust. Add another pie crust on top and brush whipped egg over top to add shine to crust. Bake on 300 for 90 minutes until crust is brown.

Ingredients for 2 pie shells:

2 cups of self rising flour

½ tsp salt

1tbsp of sugar

½ cup of shortening

½ cup of cold water

Directions for 2 pie shells: In a large bowl, add flour, salt, sugar, cut in shortening and then gradually start adding water into mixture with fork (until mixture resembles coarse crumbs) Lightly flour wax paper, Roll out pastry with roller pin about 1/8" thick. Flip pastry (using wax paper) over one hand and place in baking pan.

Sweet Potato Pie

When most people think of Southern baking they think of sweet potato pie. Growing up we all could not wait to go to grandmother's house to eat some of that sweet southern goodness.

Cooking time: 60 minutes

Feeds 6 -8 people

Ingredients

3-5 med size potatoes
2 whipped eggs
1 ½ cup of sugar
1 stick of butter
1 tsp of vanilla
A dash of cinnamon
A dash of nutmeg
8 oz of evaporated or condensed milk
1 tsp of flour
1 tsp of lemon extract
1 tsp of almond extract
2 pie shells

This recipe was given to me by Aunt Dot and it is dedicated to all Grandmas' out there. We love you!

Directions:

Rinse sweet potatoes and boil or bake (45-60 minutes) until potatoes are soft inside. Peel off outer skin of potatoes and add butter. Mash together and add one whipped egg and remaining ingredients. Blend together and pour inside pie shell. Add other pie crust on top and brush whipped egg across top crust to give it a glossy look. Bake on 350 for 25-30 minutes or until pie crust is golden brown. Serve with whipped or ice cream on top.

Pecan Pie

Ingredients
1 cup of light brown sugar
2 large eggs
1 stick of butter
1 ½ tsp of vanilla
1 tbsp of self rising flour
1 cup of pecans pieces
½ cup of sugar
2 tbsp of milk
9 inch deep pie shell

We have the pleasure to having this tasty delight during winter holidays and special occasions. My sister Tia would make it from scratch. **Directions:** Preheat oven to 325 degrees. Mix brown sugar, granulated sugar and eggs until creamy. Add ¾ cup of chopped pecans, melted butter, milk, flour and vanilla extract and mix. Pour mixture into pie shell. Arrange ¼ cup of pecans halves on top of pie. Bake for 55 minutes. Pie should be firm with only a slight jiggle in center. Let cool before serving.

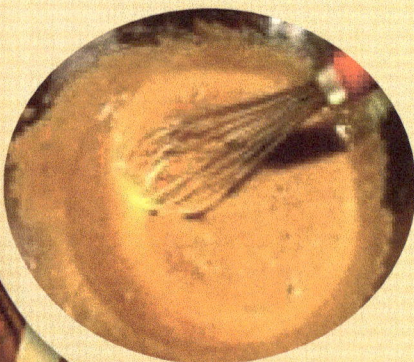

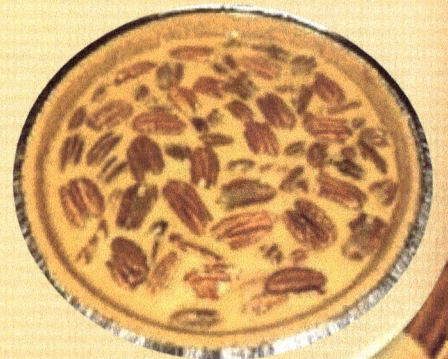

Bread Pudding

Bread pudding is another Low county favorite. It has a unique taste and texture that just reminds you of the old days. Every bite is full of goodness. Bread pudding was a dish made out of ripe fruit and old bread. Back in those days, nothing was wasted. This is another recipe is by Cousin Mildred.

Ingredients
1 loaf of bread
1 tsp of cinnamon
1 whipped egg
¾ cup of sugar
(sweeten to taste)
½ stick of butter
¼ cup milk
10 oz fruit cocktail or peaches
or any fruit chunks
½ cup raisins or nuts (optional)
¼ cup water

Directions:
In a large bowl crumble bread in pieces. Blend all ingredients together with bread and soak for 1-2 hours. Spray or grease/flour pan and bake on 350 for 90 minutes or until brown. I like to eat it warm out the oven.

Peach Cobbler

Ingredients
20 oz canned peaches or
5 peaches cut into chunks
1 tsp of cinnamon
1 cup of sugar
(sweeten to taste)
1 block of butter
1 cup milk
1 cup Jiffy baking mix
1 tsp vanilla

I was fortunate to grow up being able to go into my grandparent's backyard to pick almost any fruit I wanted. They had apple, pear, peach, several plum, cherry and pecan trees.

Directions: In a large bowl mix baking mix, sugar, melted butter, milk and vanilla until smooth. Place peach chunks across the bottom baking pan. Pour mixture on top of peaches. Sprinkle cinnamon over cobbler. Bake on 350 for 45 minutes or until golden.

37

Cornbread

Ingredients:
1 cup of self rising flour
1 cup of yellow cornmeal
1 stick of butter
¾ cup sugar
¾ cup of milk
2 eggs

Cornbread has been a tradition of soul food since the Gullah people arrived in Charleston. Cornbread or sweetbread is good tasting, fills you up, easy to prepare and most of all inexpensive. Mother said that they had sweetbread for lunch every day on their summertime visits to her Grandparents farm in Edisto Island, SC. I can still remember the good times I had as a child visiting them every Sunday after church.

Directions: Put all ingredients inside a med size bowl. Mix together and pour inside a greased floured baking pan. Bake for 40-45 minutes or until top is golden.

Momma Biscuits

Ingredients:
2 ½ cups of flour
1 tsp of baking powder
1 tsp of sugar (if desire)
½ cup of Crisco shortening
¾ cup of butter milk

Aunt Cecelia's Buttermilk Biscuits

Directions: Add flour, sugar, baking powder and milk in bowl, mix in shortening with a knife or fork (until mixture resembles coarse crumbs). Place pastry mix on lightly floured wax paper and roll out with roller pin to about ½"- ¾ " thick. Cut out dough using biscuit cutter or top rim of glass or cup. Place dough on greased pan or cookie sheet. Brush lightly with melted butter. Place in oven at 450 degrees for 10-15 min or until top is light brown.

My cousin Kevin makes the best homemade biscuits. He was lucky to get his mother's recipe. My mother told me she made the most amazing biscuits.

Pound Cake

You would never believe a slice of cake could have so many flavors until you have tried one of Cousin Shirley's cakes. Cousin Shirley sells all types of cakes for events, parties, and special occasions. You will never want another store bought cake after you devour hers.

Ingredients:
2 ½ cup self rising flour
2 ½ sticks of butter
2 ½ cup sugar
(sweeten to taste)
8 oz cream cheese
1 tbsp of vanilla
1 tbsp of rum extract
6 large eggs or 7 med
¼ tsp of salt
1 tbsp of sour cream

Directions:
Mix butter, sugar, cream cheese, vanilla, rum extract, and eggs together. In a separate bowl, mix flour, salt and baking powder.

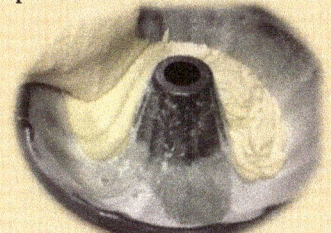

Add flour mixture and sour cream to batter. Blend with mixer or hand until batter is smooth. Pour batter inside a greased & floured baking tube pan. Preheat oven to 325 and bake for 1 hour and 15 minutes or until top is golden brown. Let cool for 25 min flip from pan and serve.

39

Blackberry Dumplings

My Grandaunt Dot fashioned this wonderful dessert during blackberry season in the spring. When I was young my brother and I would accompany my mother to gather wild blackberries from the field next door to my grandparent's house. We would get a big bag and then mix it with a little sugar to make a tasty snack. Mom would tell us how much she enjoyed Aunt Dot's blackberry dumpling as a kid. Years later Aunt Dot shared her famous springtime recipe.

Cooking time: 30 minutes
Feeds 4 -6 people

Ingredients
12 oz of Blackberries
1 cup of sugar
1 stick of butter
1 tbsp of vanilla
1 cup shortening
3 cups of water
2 ¼ cups of self-rising flour

Directions for sauce
Bring 3 cups of water to a boil and add butter, sugar and vanilla. Rinse berries with water and add to water mixture. Cook for 10 minutes and reduce heat to med low.

Directions for dumplings: Mix shortening, flour and ¾ cup of cold water together with a fork until dough beads. Increase heat to medium and scoop out little balls with a tablespoon. Add dough balls to hot blackberry mix and cook for 15 min or until balls float meaning it is done inside. Remove dumplings from sauce and pour excess sauce over dumplings.

Boiled Peanuts

Boiled Peanuts Cooking time: 3-4 hours or 1 ½ hours in pressure cooker. **Ingredients:** 2 lbs of raw peanuts, ½ to ¾ cup salt (season to taste) for Cajun add ½ cup of Cajun seasonings or for Gullah add ½ cup of Palmetto blend to water.

Directions: Rinse peanuts to remove dirt. Place peanuts and desired amount of salt in stock pot with 4 to 5 qt of water. Bring to a boil over high heat for 45 min and reduce heat to med high and cook for an additional 3 hrs or until peanuts are tender.

Fried Okra Cooking time: 20 minutes Feeds 5-6 people **Ingredients:** 20 pods of okra sliced ¼ inch, 2 eggs beaten, 1 ¼ cup of cornmeal, 1 tsp of Palmetto Blend or ½ tsp each of salt and pepper and 1 cup of Oil. **Directions:** In a bowl soak okra in egg for 5-10 minutes. Combine cornmeal and seasonings and drench okra. Place okra in hot oil and stir constantly. Cook for 5 to 10 minutes or until golden.

Fried Green Tomatoes Cooking time: 30 minutes Feeds 4-5 **Ingredients:** 3-4 med tomatoes sliced 1/8 inch, 2 eggs beaten, 1 cup of cornmeal and 1 cup flour, 1 tbsp of Palmetto Blend or 1 tsp each of salt and pepper (season to taste) and 2 cups of oil. **Directions:** In a bowl soak tomatoes in eggs for 5 minutes. Combine cornmeal, flour and seasonings. Drench tomatoes and place tomatoes in hot oil and stir constantly. Cook for 6 - 10 min or until golden. Sprinkle salt on top. Serve with ranch dressing.

Deviled Eggs Cooking time: 20 minutes feeds 5-6 people **Ingredients:** 6 boiled eggs, 1 tsp each of mayonnaise, relish and mustard. ½ stock of celery, ½ tsp of salt and pepper or Palmetto Blend (season to taste)

Directions: Slice boiled eggs in half. Take out egg yolks and mix in a bowl with the mayonnaise, relish, and diced celery. Scoop up the mixture and place inside egg whites. Sprinkle a little seasoning or paprika on top.

Sweet potato roll-ups This treat was created by my son, Kalfoni, who wanted a healthy and tasty snack. **Ingredients:** 3 sweet potatoes ¾ cup honey, ½ cup nuts, Add water as needed

Preheat oven 170. Boil potatoes until soft. Peel and put into mixing bowl. Add honey and blend together. Add water to soften mixture. Spread thin mixture on flat baking pan. Add nuts on top. Bake for 16-24 hours or until dark brown and all moisture has evaporated. Let cool and slice 2 inch strips and roll.

41

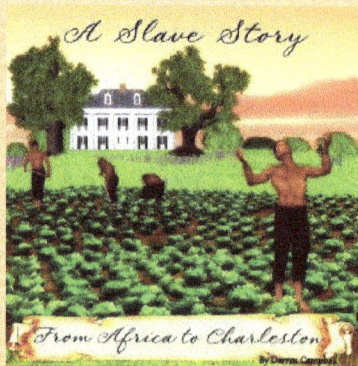

www.ingramcontent.com/pod-product-compliance
Lightning Source LLC
Chambersburg PA
CBHW040303100426
42811CB00011B/1346